Fried Fish and Flour Biscuits

MOLLY MCGLENNEN was born and raised in Minneapolis, Minnesota and is of Anishinaabe and European descent. She is an Assistant Professor of English and Native American Studies at Vassar College. McGlennen's poetry and scholarship is widely anthologized. Simon Ortiz calls *Fried Fish and Flour Biscuits* "food for our struggle and food for our victory as Indigenous people."

Fried Fish and Flour Biscuits

MOLLY MCGLENNEN

SALT

LONDON

PUBLISHED BY SALT PUBLISHING
Dutch House, 307–308 High Holborn, London WC1V 7LL United Kingdom

© Molly McGlennen, 2010

Salt Publishing 2010

Printed and bound in the United States by Lightning Source Inc.

Typeset in Swift 9.5 / 13

ISBN 978 1 84471 832 0 paperback

1 3 5 7 9 8 6 4 2

Contents

Acknowledgements

I am grateful to the editors of the following journals and anthologies in which these poems first appeared or were re-printed: *Atlantis: A Women's Studies Journal, Frontiers: A Journal of Women Studies, Santa Clara Review, Sentence: A Journal of Prose Poetics, Studies in American Indian Literatures, To Topos Poetry International: Ahani — Indigenous American Poetry, Walrus* and *Yellow Medicine Review*. "10 Little Indians", "Synonymous", "Composition" and "Legend" are found within my longer poetic essay entitled "She's Nothing Like We Thought" which was published in *Genocide of the Mind: New Native American Writing*.

Thank you to the following people who believed in me and my ability to tell these stories: Janet McAdams, Gordon Henry, Inés Hernández-Ávila, Sandra McPherson, Elizabeth Willis, and Dallas Boggs.

Thank you to those who've surrounded me with compassion and friendship along the way — from Minneapolis, to Oakland, to New York. Thank you to my colleagues who've supported me — from Mills, to Davis, to Vassar. Each of you has created for me a home away from home.

Thank you to all the folks who've invited me to read my work, and who have listened to my poetry.

Thank you to my family for entrusting me with these stories.

Thank you to Winston and Ellia for being patient and supportive — and for keeping me laughing.

Preface

Our lives are made up of recipes. Poetry is a way to preserve and translate those recipes, those stories that we hear in bits and pieces and we never stop telling. Poems are what nourish us.

The best recipes are the ones we know by heart, the ones we fight to remember because when we follow them, we are drawing together many different elements from our life.

Lives-made-of-recipes. For me poetry is a way to process, to remember those stories I heard growing up and I continue to hear. Some stories I still haven't heard completely or never will. Still, they are there. Maybe, as Janice Gould says, they lay beneath our hearts. Or maybe, those guidelines-for-living are always out in front of us, placed there by our ancestors.

The voice in my poetry is many people and things at once. And because of this, poetry is best served aloud. One of my favorite things is to read poems to people. To see their faces. In those moments, I can give the poems away.

Voices from an array of people have lived in the poems even before they were ever written down. They are there, shaping the design of the poem and encoding their messages.

Though I'm sure this has been said before, these words are not mine alone. I do not think I'd have the courage to write poems if it weren't for family members (particularly from a legacy of women) and a great many poets who have informed my creativity. Writers like Luci Tapahonso, Kim Blaeser, Elizabeth Woody, Diane Glancy, Simon Ortiz, Deborah Miranda, Gordon Henry, Chrystos, Gerald Vizenor, Joy Harjo and Wendy Rose have articulated in one way or another that poetry is a form of community-building, a means to locate oneself in relationship to a network of people and places and memories.

That is why so many of my poems are dedicated to or written for other people. Poetry is connection; it's what allows us to travel to other people, to say hello, to honor. And, by those networks of connection, we find our paths of continuance... through urban streets and northern lakes, loneliness and companionship, through failure and balance, toward a creative spirit that nourishes us all.

With the following poems I honor my maternal grandmother who passed away in the final stages of this collection coming together. She is and always has been the progenitor of my words and my creative spirit.

To-Do List Before Writing a Poem:

Recall the words we want her to teach
nookomis, niigiizis, zaaga'igan.
Affix them to photos,
the picture-words imagined in blood.

Trace the footprints of shadows.
The way she washes her hair at night
in lakes that have always bathed us—
children asleep, four to a room.

Build the house again. Creak of floorboards,
birchbark cauldron to hold manomin,
a butter moon
to say it's going to be fall.

Feel her wrist and forearms ache.
The years of rolling out
biscuits and scrubbing screen doors.
Her days of cradling.

Name the sons she buried early:
one's decay in the VA hospital
agent-orange-riddled; the other crashing
to asphalt, atonement.

Listen when she says.

Evince the scars.

Return.

Legend

My body remembers
the time we rolled out dough
for two days.
Flour hands
salted heat
a kitchen like fire.
Careful not to pat it
too thin,
biscuits should fill
empty stomachs
you tell me.
No more school
after fourth grade—
what's a little girl to do
but listen
and follow the mark
of a hand,
hear a history
punctuated by story,
when your mother
would whisper hers
in between scaling
and gutting
the walleye,
ashamed to admit
how lakes
had always fed her family
how she had married
a pale Frenchman
moved away from the water.
So you
a daughter once removed
now stands next to me—
says history doesn't have to mean
coming over in a boat,

says this is how
you feed a family:
until your hands and arms ache
until your body remembers
the blood in its lines
like fried fish
and flour biscuits.

Living the Language

She tells us the Ojibwe word for blueberry pie
is the recipe to make it:
miibashkimiinasigunbatagiingwesijiiganbiitooingwesijiiganibakwezhigan

as we pick the delicate fruit from each calyx
indigo bulb hanging from a perfect five-pointed star
a gift to relieve our hunger—
selecting each one, each star-berry staining our fingers purple-red.
We can't help but pop some in our mouths.

She had said the juice could cure a cough
and the leaves could be tea—would be good for our blood.
        In the summers they'd dry them and store for long winters.

We trod through marshy ground searching for the next lowbush
can taste the pie already, baking slowly in her stove
can see her careful thumbs creating the wave that edges the crust
sliding the fork through the top in four directions
holes for breath

as we punch ours out now—blueberry hunting.
We are this language of progression, this recipe
renewed each time our pails are filled and
our fingers drip hard blood in gratitude at the end of days.

Dream Song

You say poetry
like dream
is visited
by people
and their stories—
shadows of
who we are.
A deck of grandkids
shuffling around
a tatty card table,
aunties and their rhythmic hands,
your cribbage board and
Camel cigarettes.
Pepsi from the bottle.
We laugh at the railing
over a swamp full
of cattails
and crickets—
all that keeps us busy
arranges us
in song.
Inside, someone
plinks out
Johnny Cash
Willie Nelson
your favorites
cuz they're In'dan ya' know.
You sing us
into the evening
when we fall
asleep in the backs
of old cars

and recover these days
that are greater than
any of us
alone.

Learning Irony in Order

First grade and the nun tells us to sit
indian-style in a circle
upon a rust scrap of nylon rug —
we dash to find a spot
that is not stained
drop down playing dead —
then situate ourselves
negotiating space.
I try to claim my territory
in her blindspot
that way I can wiggle all I want to
make faces at her
safe in my allotment.

She bawls at us
sit still
keep our hands in our laps
and pay attention
while my mind rides a horse
kicking dust:
I'm no longer in my plaid green jumper
and white pressed shirt
no longer in my itchy socks —
my two braids unravel.

I think of the day he joined our class
when they laughed at his long thick braid
(while I secretly loved it and mine)
mocked his name
Sol
(while I danced in it)
and sneered the morning he came to the circle
with his hair cut short —
Sister Clairine thought it best he fit in
now a citizen of the group.

Order makes us closer to god.

I'm corralled into the present
with her shots to tame down
find myself in Angel of God
he alongside me in unison
each tilling our space,
showing her we're farmers of prayer
planting *ever this day be at my side*
amidst our shame.

I'll never know if he cried
when the blade hit
if he knew that I'd give him mine if I could
everyday sitting indian-style
living our parceled lives.

Our Hands

Precious stones fasten deep inside where stories are told
ones that start with definitions
what one color means as opposed to another
thick hands strong with age   extend beyond your heart
as if they have history written out on them
an old brown woman sells corn on a corner
a son dies soon with clay for skin
a granddaughter will write this down
tie stories to fingers   so you do not forget   feel the tug of a hand
when you are tired and want to forget
pick up the stones again   remember in pieces
remember how those stones felt   as they sank in your hands.

What Red Leads To

In the mirror I read my face backward, blood inscription of my name
engraved within the lines that figure my nose and chin—that tiny
place above my lip, a bowl for tears.
Pressing my face closer I ride the indigo veins circumventing
my eyes, spaces of navigation, but it's all spiraling:

Like the day I helped her peel potatoes, the skins curling down
into a blueberry kitchen sink; we were both barefoot
and the July heat blasted
through the screens, a rusted oscillating fan turned on our legs
every nine seconds (I was counting),

sometimes backwards, the games I'd play in my head,
the vast amounts
of silence innate to a mother and daughter.
We'd shift our weight as she wondered when my father'd be home,
as I tried to translate the words that buzzed out from the fan's cage.
Did it say "stopping now," "almost wrong," "you're so dumb?"

Everything was unwinding: earlier,
the neighbor-girl and I played dress-up
in the backyard for an audience of rocks who
would see me dismount my too-large platform heels,
watch my unraveling crimson gypsy blouse, the one
I usually tied like a halter-top

because at lunch she had said I was a sexpot and squeezed
her eight-year-old eyes at me like almost-dead roses, the ones
on our kitchen table, blackened and shriveled—
how that morning I woke from a dream about rooms flooded with red,
ran to the mirror looking for a different
face, that morning, when the petals had pooled
around the vase
in a thousand directions.

How to Make Rock Soup

In September
take 3 or 4 smooth clean rocks
from behind the house
about the size of medium potatoes.
From the kitchen,
1 large onion the size of his fist
and 3 tomatoes,
the ones we find fat at the end of summer,
dice and sing:
> *Set out, paddle across midnight water*

Cut up 3 carrots, a stalk of celery
add a scoop of butter
some corn, about as much as can be held
in the small yellow bowl
and say:
> *This song is your guide*

Sprinkle 3 fingers of salt and pepper
the way he'd dip into his can of snuff
or clasp the switch on the fan,
a kitchen grows warm with prayer:
> *Hear us when you're approaching shore*

As we boil our kettle-full of water
rocks settled along the bottom
small memorials to him
we add the rest and sing:
> *Remember us long after dawn*

Later, pull the rocks and wash them
set aside and save wrapped in a white cloth
serve the soup with the flour biscuits he loved.

A Trail of Devotion

For my Grandfather

His Camel flickers
between carameled finger and thumb
as he swivels his chair
allowing the view
to the old highway—
        drone of cars
        like a lullaby of days.
He counts minutes
with sips from his whiskey, feet resting
upon a tired green floor.

Before bed
he will empty his pockets
from the day—
        a carving knife
        four quarters
        silver lighter
then wash his hands,
try to rinse away calluses and cuts
as if night will bring mending

to years of delivering
        tuxedo-armed sofas
        canopy beds
        cherry veneer queen annes
to the houses of people
who avert their eyes and warn
him to wipe his feet.

He knows his limits in these places.

At the window
he lines his finger along
a stained table top, the one
that holds eight children
and an evening prayer,
the one they crowd around to tell
the stories that stitch the days together.
      The way the cars will buzz along
      seamlessly.

For Uncle
(Richard Joseph Roskop 1951–1991)

You don't even look
like the rest of the eight.
Dark sand for skin, hair to mid-back.
You let my brother and me throw rocks
at cars, eye sores in your idealistic vision.
One for agent orange.
One for those god damned politicians.
One because.

And you talk funny —
a nasal buzz.
We didn't know that illness hides
behind a wide-eyed stare. You hitchhike through
the Badlands, search for medicine your mother told you about
stories revealed in dreams,
camp at Pike's Peak with smoke
and clouds, find a wife under a rock.

I get caught in your stare
then unleashed with a wink
while my brother wears your sailor cap
and makes the peace sign.
You seek the sun, roam alongside eagle,
pine needles and frost on the ground.
A thin body shakes bleak thoughts.

Then at last I remember:
you and I and my brother on a green couch
in that apartment on E. 22nd,
leaves on a vine.
I couldn't say the word peyote,
never heard of a VA hospital —
only knew what I saw
cigarette fingers
and a red bandana on your head.

Hair gone
another piece stripped from you.
Beads hang from a doorway.

Only now can I pronounce adrenoleukodistrophy
or understand chemical agents.
So I trace your memory here in this dirt, with this rock,
with these helpless hands.

In Spirit

Native and non-Native people from around the country participated in "The Longest Walk" of 1978 as demonstration to end "the most evil US policies"—government seizure of Native lands not protected by treaty without due process of law or compensation.

Aligned within their cadence of sleep
I lie safe.
They—like two drums—
pound my life's pulse
as the tired transistor radio
voices a local broadcast
    Some 30,000 Indians
    starting in California
    march across the country.

Here in the dark
with the night turned on its back,
a horizon of dreams as our dance begins.

I move between them in circles
    The largest gathering
    of Native People this century
as we had looked through old pictures
in her kitchen earlier—
the sun warming its way in.
Mid-afternoon slows
our breathing.

Find myself within story
alongside the woman smoking pipe
along the water
that bathed and fed them.

She will cook into the evening
as they pen their declaration
    "Today we pray
    for the coming generations"
while I ready for bed once again
days as backdrop
I shed my skin
climb between them as always.

Five hundred years spill outside my window.
Stars snared in my vigil
I will dance all night—
our own drum sending a prayer
ribbons tied round my song.

Shanawdithit, the Last Beothuk

Shanawdithit was the last remaining Beothuk, a tribe in the Newfoundland area of Canada. Their extinction marks one of the cruelest fates suffered by indigenous Americans. Captured in 1823, Shanawdithit was taken to the Beothuk Institution to be studied and "civilized." It was here that she drew dozens of maps and sketches depicting nearly all the information non-Natives have of the Beothuk tribe and the genocide committed against them. She died of tuberculosis in 1829.

They graph lines that strangle our throats
measure out a Beothuk's savagery with a key
to illustrate tuberculosis by north
starvation by west and a reward of 100 pounds for our capture
all depicted to scale
a need to scalp such wildness—
expansion can be contained to a piece of paper, they say.

We follow caribou amidst the interior of what they call Newfoundland
camp along lakes and rivers
aligning and dismantling bands that will form
no trade relations with them—
by then we knew the beast that stalked on haunches
and carried fire of disease and a righteous god.

They branded us "Red Indian" and tracked us
framing maps to parcel and divide
for three decades justified ownership
as only written documents are able.

But I transpose my culture as an artist would
an ever-changing refrain of shoreline and rock
my pencil's coal charts the reflection
of how we crushed ocher under early-morning sun
and mixed it with oil or grease
rubbed our bodies and heads
a ritual steeped in mothers and daughters, our protection.

My maps chart my mother, sister and me
gathering mussels from the bay
weakened by foodless stomachs
captured to live among colonists
where, for six years, I compose my story by hand:
from thousands of us to one
each drawing an act of survival
as I remember those gone now
and I, too, will soon pass
breath of the Beothuk blows fierce with each lesion-filled lung.

To look for parallels is to miss the mark.
My landscapes are in my mother's hands
holding a shoe-wan to her lips.
My drawings narrate how
my aunt, Demasduit, in the midst of a massacre
bared her milk-filled breasts to the captors
as a plea to spare her baby.

Trace our stories not with ruler or compass
but as the herds of caribou that fed my people:
unrestricted by boundaries
we will live beyond the date that slates our demise.

War Curio

*During the aftermath of the Wounded Knee Massacre of 1890, an infant survivor
was found and taken by General William Colby against the will of the few surviving
Lakota. Raised by the General's family, Lost Bird was his "display piece for profit."
She died in Los Angeles in 1920. Not until 1991 did the Lakota obtain the rights to
her remains to rebury her at the Wounded Knee Memorial mass gravesite.*

Lost Bird, find your way
alongside your buried family
in the killing field of one hundred years ago
where the survivors were hunted down and executed
because the blood running in their veins was Indian
as editorials solicited wholesale extermination
by laws of conquest
"beloved justice prevails with civilization."

You fly now, Lost Bird
amongst children left for dead
wrapped in the shawls of their frozen mothers
a red coat of snow smothering the bodies
who had gathered to dance and pray in open-air circles.

Lost Bird, you—little girl child—
who was found unharmed,
adopted by the army officer
his bric-a-brac for show
for profit
"A genuine Indian"
displayed to no fewer than 500 of his closest friends.

Lost Bird, his newly acquired possession,
you sing the remnants of your mothers
surrounded by soldiers despite their flags of truce
fired upon
despite the babies in their arms despite
their promised safety.

You no longer need to entertain, Lost Bird
as you were put on display
in Buffalo Bill's Wild West
authentic, exotic
torn from the carnage
to serve as the reason for his destruction
epitome of savagery.

At 29, filled with disease, in a place so far from your own
Lost Bird, did you hear your people's call
The whole world is coming
singing into a trance
their backs to the line of Hotchkiss.

Lost Bird, you carry a message
you—Zintka Lanuni, Lakota—
dance with them now, Messenger to the spirit world
you rise in their sacred circle.

At the Oakland Indian Charter School
For Rosa

She strains with pencil in hand
carving a foreign language
as if she dripped paint from a brush
not the words her own mother spoke:
Choctaw—traditions based in story.
The other documents progress
date by date
a progression of events, watches
her mouth whisper
"I don't know how to read"
as if she lived a life in that half-second.
Words past   now   and forward
in one circle
a lesson of doing
stumbling across a lesson to sound it out.
There, in that old building
called a school
where textbooks don't explain her story,
history is not linear.
She is a mother at eleven
baby growing without her
back in Mississippi.
Now she must muscle through pages
of scattered memory
pull these pictures together and
envision her dreams onto the paper.
This is where she begins a poem—
in between her words.

Tour Guide
For Sarah Bad Heart Bull, Oglala Sioux

In Custer, South Dakota
visit an Indian village:
"Come See How They Live"
>   *where in February, 1973*
>   *below freezing*
>   *she joins more than 200*
>   *around the courthouse*
>   *to await the verdict*

In Custer, read about the Battle
at Little Big Horn
how the man himself
made his last stand in these hills
>   *while they drum and sing war songs*
>   *chant hoka-hay*
>   *as her son's murderer is acquitted*

Custer, where a saloon's sign reads
"No Indians and Dogs Allowed"
>   *(because Wesley Bad Heart Bull,*
>   *the freed Wasicun screams,*
>   *needed to be taught a lesson)*

Custer, where the 1868 Fort Laramie Treaty
was ignored because of reported gold,
forgotten after Wounded Knee
>   *as they club her down*
>   *choke her with a riot stick*
>   *pressed against the throat*
>   *snow as heavy as swift justice*

See the pageant "How The West Was Won"
tour John Wayne country
>In Custer, bleeding and naked
>she's dragged through the street by police
>where she sits in a jail cell
>having made herself a nuisance
>over her son's death

Custer "The Town With the Gunsmoke Flavor"
>where she echoes
>the sacred thunderbird legend
>deep inside the Paha Sapa.

Maneuvering Targets

After Jim Goldberg's Exhibit "Raised by Wolves" at San Francisco's Modern Museum of Art, September 1997.

The manipulation of camera
like the anthropologist
who poses the native for
something other than truth.
A depiction
based upon
an artist's intentions.

One feels the lens
as a piercing eye—
with a snap
one world
collapses
on another.

And when the boy
who was shot by his own father
stands with a stitched
stomach toward the aperture,
one wonders
how this precision
is revealed.

Left to the viewer
the story is told
through a maneuvering hand—
a photo
narrowed
by its interpretation.

Is it the way
the photographer
kneels
down
in front of the ribbed body
adjusting the focus
as if to repent?

Or is it the way
a letter lies
below the photo
crinkled and vulnerable,
a small manifesto
unleashing
at last his reality.

Silent Death

For Kevin Cooper
Slated for execution 12:01am, February 10, 2004

A black luster of crows travels over
San Quentin, their caws swing down
through heavy iron gates, locked—
no one to hear them or him
haaa haaa haaa.
What it must sound like to exhale
the smells of shit and piss
and the waste of twenty impenetrable years.
What it must sound like to pen your innocence
on the cement walls of cells,
to see the lines of your face grow graver
towards the thought of it:
a grave for a forgotten body, useless, rotting
while feathered black sheen, a murder
of crows circles and squawks, twenty more hours
to listen, but no one will listen.
They are the droning that deadens the hundreds of bodies
amassed outside the barbwire.
Inside he'll wait, twenty more hours
to listen, a chamber awaits with chairs for watching death
—just as the one surviving victim had watched twenty years ago
on the hospital television—
the suspect's picture flashing across its screen
and the little boy in his bed uttering:
that's not him.

Paper Hearts

For too many women

She remembers the months marked by holidays
valentines meant February
when she'd fold red construction paper in half
cut an angel's wing and open
a see-through heart.

It wasn't so much the love that had fallen away
like the angel cast from heaven,
stories that nuns would dictate
while she colored red hearts within the lines—

but now, as she is crying in the clinic,
he waiting with her, something stirring inside,
she is reminded of the hearts she used to draw
and the blood she's about to spill;
this time the cut will leave more than a hole.

Somehow they fold together there
if just for those next few hours,
she is one wing, he the other—
something will be torn from them both,
and later they, too, will be severed.

She was once told that everyone has guardian angels
who would help scissor straight and color neatly,
but as she walks in the room, places legs
in the stirrups, hers hides behind
the doctor's sterile tray of instruments.

These aren't the holy days she remembers—
she sees the paper hearts scatter on the floor,
her angel falling with them.

Once She Was a Ghost

for Halloween
old white bed sheet
two scissored eyes
and a rubberband
around her neck
let free to roam
streets riddled
with trees
dark thin fingers
just her
hit every house
between second
and fifth
wet leaves piled
on the boulevard
as her mask
grows damp
from punched-out breaths.
Now she walks
a different street
triggered with concrete
trees gone
replaced with puffs
of smoke
phantoms lurk
ask her to stop
in her path
hand over those treats
barrel points between
what was once
cut out holes.

Double Vision

There are limits to these situations
where the whole of a person
rests opposite another.
Eyes sigh across a table.
The unfolding begins and
they are caught there
unable to rehearse the ordinary—
the same scenery still
moves by them
but their eyes, now hooks,
gouge the edges of view.

Swallowing Her Words

If anything, she'll eat these words someday.
Who'd believe a girl who scribbles and types alone
about *all her relations*, living or dead,
a life consisting of photos
kept in a manila envelope,
stories of coca cola and corned beef n' cabbage,
her trips to Big Sandy, Pulaski, Shady Oak.
The constant chatter of water that keeps her afloat,
thinking that someday she'd score this noise.

Do you see the absurdity?
All the metaphors in the world
can't bring them to her, can't make her
swallow these little black symbols
that mark pitch and tempo, sheet music
she keeps finding in the belly of a dusty piano bench—
songs she'll inhabit for days.

And if anything, she'll be caught choking.

But sometimes words are all she has to live on—
and the memories
that flesh her fully.

Columbus Day

I have been told the secrets of never having a home.

A history of fallen oak and pine needles returns our lives.

Now they must sneak wild rice at the foot of the bluff.

The phone call tells you someone has died,
      I've witnessed too many of these.
      She hums show tunes and hands
      out holy cards.

And somehow he knew to give the blanket
      to my mom; now she gives it to me,
      the one on my bed.
      I know the story behind that, too.

Grandkids spit pits from the dock, watch future
      fruit float ashore. We've always been here.

Work dough to tableside. Aprons tell stories.
I bear the markings.

Composition

I assemble with the hands of a poet
who does not know the end
of her poem, ink is an afterthought.
Piecing myself together I use all the material I can gather:
Potter's clay and her acrylic paints, thick and thin
camel-hair brushes; a chinese jump rope that noosed my ankles,
twine we used to hold the tomato plants.
If I use food, it's mostly
what I can recall: Wild rice and walleye,
peeled oranges left for me in the morning.
The crescent-moon cashews she loves.
If I need markers, I locate northern lakes,
lilac bushes that guarded our back yard,
overgrown and drooping with fragrance:
The cotton-blue bed sheets she draped on the line.
I must sit patiently to do this, to place it all in order,
from memory. But will it matter
if I can't quite get the smell—
her hands as they tied ribbon round ends of my braids?

What Holds Us

I am waiting for the words to come from you
float to me in the half-sleep that rides on the bulbs of rain
streaming outside, can hear them hit the roof,
drip down the sides, plant themselves,
you to me, our edges touch.

Pull photos out, see the tarpaper shack
behind you and your sister
posing, squinting toward the midday sun
wonder who took the shot, told you not to smile,
or was that your choice? Square to the lens with your best dress,
worn and wrinkled from bending and hauling buckets
of water from the well, boiling the rocks for soup
and only what was left: an old potato, soft onion
or carrot—peels of things—filling the kettle, their stomachs,
no matter.

Each time I'm full. Somehow, your palms callused
and tired, bring me this. Outside the rain falls
in layers: potato, onion, carrot skins,
the casings that hold me to you.

Preparing for Flight

Sitting at the edge
of a bed
she watches me
fold my life
into a suitcase.
Alone in her own
apartment now
so nice to visit
before you go
Misses the every-
day of cooking
and feeding
a family,
the thumping of feet
at a kitchen doorway
what else do you need
to eat before
your flight

Not enough time.
I can't find
my earrings
say a little
prayer to St. Jude
patron saint
of hopeless cases
gives me an angel pin
to attach to my bra strap—
the closest place
to my heart.

I'm almost finished
and she upstairs
frying bologna
store bread
will have to do
a voice while I eat
telling me
she hates to fly
as if she's asking
me to never leave.
The cold metal
of the pin
against my chest—
its sharp edge
slitting her words open
bare as bloodlines.

Letter

I will be remembered in a Novena of masses, first nine days of September, the advent of another school year, but I am no longer in school. She keeps me in patterns of memory, tucked between rosary beads and holy water, as if I were preparing for first holy-communion once again.

The day I wore tiny white carnations and baby's breath. A saint card from her in my gloved hands, signed sweetly in that same motion of familiarity: *Love and prayers, Only me.*

She's crafted 1,000 of these, sitting window side, writing notes to her grandchildren, with each a holy card attached, marked *a little prayer for you.*

In this one from the Divine Savior, she pens right under the "Amen," *you can hang this up on the fridge.* And I will try to recall what the INRI means above Christ's head, will try to recall those bodies of words between us.

Letter II

Got another letter from her the other day and attached in this one, a valentine novena in the shape of a book mark. For the next nine days I will be "graced by the knowledge of God's spirit." Signed, *Love you, grandma.* I notice the lower-case g, directly below "in Jesus' name we pray."

Sorry I'm slow in answering, my excuse is not a happy one. Toby died, went to the funeral in Colorado Springs. And here, as if to pause to send a little prayer, she adds *the weather was warm, but on the day of the mass it snowed.*

All the grandkids are getting sick, but not me; only, my knee hurts because the weather is changing so much. Like ma used to say, 'it's hell gettin' old.' I picture her as she laughs at herself, makes me laugh all over, because I see her wide smile, her thick hand slapping her knee.

I tuck the letter back in its envelope, and place it in the box that holds our years together. I will write her today and ask her again about her mother: Grandma, tell me once more how she made you kids wear the big hats in summertime; tell me once more how she taught you to laugh in spite of yourself, the trick to understanding those midday shadows.

The Dance

She knows the length of each day
in shadow-slants across her bare floor.
They grow longer as the pain
in both knees festers—
metal balls marbling beneath cap and skin,
jingle dress dancing
in the marrow of her bones.
She moves her chair to follow
what is left of the November sun,
closes her eyes as she has always done
to recount a story:
Standing on solid brown legs
over boiling pots of potatoes;
grandchildren at a table, some with green eyes
and some with eyes
black as magpies;
ache-less hands to weave braids
in honeyed hair, or
shuck corn in mid-July.
She raises hands like the old-time dancers.
Here, in an afternoon that extends
Itself, memory exploding through the traps
in her mind, she recalls it was four women
in the dream—
tiers of jingle cones
adorn her,
ring healing for another sacred day.

From the Kitchen

Beans are little lungs—
white and curved
before pouring them in the boil.
Grip the sides
of the pot
stir
and inhale steam.
A small rite
to follow hands
that swirl
the butter and brown sugar—
all humming in a saucepan.

Outside, a wren perches
just long enough.
His tail
upright.

If quiet is a cure,
watch how the bacon's sliced,
endure the grease. See
that these directions are small rushes
of air.
Hold your breath,
let them simmer
without a sound—
lift most from death.

Yosemite, 1976

We sit at the feet of gods
half moon rock
slicing us in two
both shirtless
bare like granite
I am no different from you
shapeless and wet
cutting through blades of grass
that grow along the river's curve
scraping bare legs
yours no more muscular than mine
we sort pebbles
gifts set out for us
stack them in piles
for sun   *for moon*   *for all that we are in*
the river swirls around us
small bodies cut from birth
not knowing the differences that will unfasten us.

Exposed

The summer my father showed me how
to plant my own morning glories
I had no idea.
Every morning I'd run outside
to catch them opening themselves
to the sun, I thought, to the glory
even if it was raining devilishly, muddying up
the yard, making it impossible
to walk without squishing black
on my white tennis shoes, even if
it was Minnesota humid, mosquitoes
out by 9am, the cicada already droning,
heat bug belting her forecast—
so hot you'll sweat in the shower—
little moons unlock their throats of white
and awake like babies
as if they'd been holding their breaths the whole night.

I had no idea
when his heart poured out to me
explaining how to prepare the soil,
turning it over and over, sprinkling cow dung;
the way he warned me
about over-watering, to steady my hand
with the garden hose; how to carve
the furrows that hold the line of seeds,
be patient with the hoe, use my whole
body and scatter the seeds evenly,
my small hands caked with our work.
In time the flowers climb their lavender bodies
up the trellis we'd assembled,
efforts of devotion.

I had no idea about the oversized valentine leaves
weighing heavy in the morning light,
the bells expanding to a whole world
of dawn, glories singing, photophilous wonders—
I see him then.
We, together, in full sun
twining their vines upward.
I had no idea his heart that he'd opened
would fail him, would close up
come evening, drawn tight in its folds and darkness
to rest.

Film Clip

She makes sure you catch
8 *feet* on Kodachrome
before she strokes across the pool
Mark this.
Warm Arizona air
hides such depths
and a red and orange 2-piece.

8 millimeters
catch each butterfly arm
2 of the same
head bowed
thumbs down draw the edges of circles,
but it isn't about the boundaries
pool decks and gutters or
you with camera in hand.

Only minutes
to catch this liquid landscape
pruned fingers and pony-tail hair.
Minutes
to catch the wide-gapped uppers
and overlapped lowers
of a smile;
the synchronization of a small dolphin,
rhythm in legs and breath

You aren't supposed to understand
when she speaks through lenses—
dust from an 8-year-old tongue
and your face in the glass—
never said anything
about what she should do

when she feels herself slipping
between
those borders again.

Reels become
clippings of indecipherable words;
on the screen, her tiny arms turning over and over
toward the wall.

Interwoven

At thirty months old a baby is exactly
one-half her adult height, you were told—

so you taught her to measure up
right, stand under a ruler
against the wall to slate
her progression over the years:

a penciled trellis of story.
How one vine slowed for a year
then shot up crazily

knees aching at night and
taller than all
the boys; a basketball always in hand.

She'd hold herself still
not to tangle or waver,
a climber perching in the earth-green
overgrowth of a smudged wall.

You'd line the rows for her:
the days she cried, hating
her hand-me-down boy-shoes
for the beginning of season,

how you'd spend the night scrubbing
and bleaching the soles and laces,
all of the halves you'd complete
before she realized.

Luminary

You were the wild one
on the front porch
with lies to pass.

Your moon mouth howling
and eyes like an August thunderstorm.
Speaking French with your mother,
surviving on Catholic charities

Stormy hair illumining northern
lake stories, the spruce's drooping cones
that line the horizons of memory.

Home late from working the bar
where you'd drink more
than a body could handle,
having to play into stranger's pockets
and seedy smiles,
you watch your baby boy and girl asleep—
two crescent bodies pulled from the heavens.

Would they hear the late-night-secrets
you whispered? A good story has no moral.
Would they know your liver gave out
before you were ready
to leave them? Before each luminary
filled the sky.

Remembering Louis
Louis Owens 1948-2002

What is it that builds a body—
old jeans and a worn wool sweater,
your brown cowboy boots?

Can it be the way you slid half
your hands in pockets
or looked up from your bifocals—
Mississippi colored eyes.

And what is it that lives around
a body? Wolf songs.

You said you could never write a poem,
there wasn't room or time enough
to hold all your desert musings
or the knowledge only mountains could sing.

Four years now
and I still hear fire fighter
stories, fly-fishing,
the rivers streaming
through all our ears.

But today, looking through
the books you'd lent to me
those I'd intended to return,
your notations in them read
like pieces of falling

trails
I will pick up—
your voice thriving
around old cars, coffee cups,
shadows of juniper, magnolia
and all such lyrical bodies.

Coming Back Round
For Ignatia Broker

"Our way of life is changing, and there is much we must accept. But let it be only the good. And we must always remember the old ways. We must pass them onto our children and grandchildren so they too will recognize the good in the new ways."

FROM *NIGHT FLYING WOMAN.*

I am a woman of mirrors
the full-length on the back of a bathroom door.
Yesterday, I see her again
silver hair, brittle legs, stockings.
Tomorrow at the university
I will teach about "story cycles' and "multiple narrators."

And I will wonder:
How many angles does one reflection make?

Young sisters jumping in heaps of leaves
see themselves for the first time in pieces.

The fall I learned to collect leaves
I'd place them between paper
transfer their veins through green crayon
like the ones in my hands
thin and busy
the only part of myself I'd study.

My mother would sit me on the rock
comb through my wet hair
weave two braids on either side
so the next day my hair would have waves—
all the while
my hands going over and over
the tracings of a leaf.

Daughters, remember your fullness.

Three Poems for Ellia

GRACE

For four days I snort and buckle in an East Oakland apartment.
During nights of toil, I swim alongside myself. Four walls burn sage.
I hang the medicine bundle he gave me. You are a small crescent
moon turning on your head. We approach winter solstice together.
A time to hear stories. I will tell you how you got your name. That
December long ago, starving, they returned home with nothing
they were promised. Unwavering. She teaches me this. The mis-
handled allotment fees. Official rolls complete with her absence.
That easily, we're erased. These tiny signatures we call names.
Finally, you come—slick black hair, my relief—inscribing us with
your long descent. Daughter, push these little words along. You, like
her, determine our worth.

Album

This poem is a box of photos. Names are photos refracted. Your hands spell our recipes. Biscuits flood morning kitchens and grandchildren's mouths. But what's in these names we've been given? What do they hold? We borrow and hate the dust that collects on bleeding tongues. What's better is smell: Blueberry pancakes. My baby-daughter's neck as she sleeps. What's better is memory: Her first kick like a cluster of ants inside my stomach. A smoothed crimson ribbon to hang. Arcs of light deviate from their path in pairs. Tear open these words. This poem is gratitude.

In Keeping

I keep lists of things for her. Lists become a mother's diary. Lilacs. Alleyways. Boulevards. Cherry blossoms. St. Francis Assisi statue. Overgrown rhubarb. Tangled tomato vines.

Lists become backyard ironies: Cutoff-shorts. Drop-lines and dug-up worms. Rusty hooks. The farmer's rock pile. Inner tubes on windy days bobbing in the lake. Raking seaweed. Picking carrots and beets for our cousins. Salting radishes.

Lists punctuate satire: Nuclear family visits Mount Rushmore. Grandmother goes to daily mass. Aluminum canoe. A Minneapolis duplex. 4th of July BBQ.

Lists mock memories: First basketball high-tops. Using a plant for a Christmas tree. Packing an old van. Leg-singeing vinyl seats. Catholic charities. Car crashes.

We will start new lists: Your days and nights mixed-up. Neighborhood fistfights. Oakland eucalyptus. A grandfather's song. Sunlight climbs into your cradle for the first time.

Each is your story.

So Many Times I Have Missed You

On our plane ride back
to San Francisco
we sit dormant beside one another
uncomfortable in our seats.
We avoid turning our heads
or touching our arms together,
dodge eye contact.
I play this game with you.
This game you invented
for times like these.

Mothers can play this game
and their mothers —
keeping themselves busy
by scrubbing the bathroom
folding laundry
washing windows,
ways to slip in and out
of rooms.
Ways to peel potatoes,
listening only to the scrape
of the knife ripping skin.

It will never be said.

You feign sleep
wrestle in your seat until we land,
exit the terminal swaggering satisfaction.
You've won.

At home we begin to fall
into what we know.
I'm on the outside
with my bucket of water,
sponge and torn rag in hand.

You stand inside
with the Windex and paper towels.
We make circles on the glass
freeing dirt
seeing only the space we make between us,
checking for streaks and lines
edges of clarity.

Later, as if we've healed,
we join ourselves to cook a dinner.
Chop peppers and onions
measure oil and salt;
set a table of mixed-matched silverware
and cups,
then sit down to eat
with wounds
festering
above our chipped plates.

At the Sushi Bar

Not even a dry spell
could make me write this

the way wasabe
unclumps in the soy sauce

the bedecking ginger
like fleshy-pink petals

not even the perforated chop
stick could inspire me,

the way you break it
in two

saki as warm as your mouth.
No, not even this

the pinguid maguro wrapped
in veiny-green foil,

how you savor the slide
down your throat

or body of avocado
embedded in coiling rice

down into the cleft
of a lubricious lobe;

I am all dried out,
even the raw oysters fail—

the ones stabbed in minced
scallions and a quail egg,

zealous as the hand
that carves them

from their pelvic shell.

Wine Tasting

They ride
in a limousine
through Napa Valley.
Merlot
1000 flowers
and a touch of oak.
Eight bottles of reds
and hours to kill.
Swirling butter and pepper
sticking to the sides,
as if they knew
what they were doing,
feigning body or
leaving tannin in their mouths.
She pricks her finger
on a broken wine glass
a small crimson bouquet drips
on her white dress,
the one she brought
with her from San Diego
the one picked out
especially for this—
and all that she can think of is the cut
the petals
of blood
that fall to her opened lap.
They term her fear
hemo-phobia
and laugh
but the nasea still churns
in her stomach,
a chalky face turned
toward blackened windows.
No one on the road
can see her

will ever know
small deaths happen
all the time.
That the consistency
of body
is blood
in her vein
the part in her lips
a slow shade in her mouth.

Weaving Water

It is enough to sew themselves together
for one night,
enough to transform a dark room into
their dreams
like the one where they swim
arm in arm—
tangled kelp at sea.
She knows this place
somewhere beside a drawer full
of letters loved and lost,
those too will be remembered—
as if they'd always visited shores
crushed with shells.
But in this fabric now
it is enough
to see the whole piece
not quite finished
as they lie in this blued space,
the color that fingers their bodies
separate
right before the sun hauls him off.
Threaded beads spill to the floor.
She will grow wise
this time, pick them up
to place in pocket
while her heart slows
to the sound of water and a rock.

Synonymous

They say in each country *la manera* is different.
Here, the shake of his shoulders
must double our rhythm of step
while Orquestra Charanzón belts a dizzying *son*.
The faster the better, I say
lo más pronto possible.
You echo me in Spanish all night
just as our bodies mirror a flawless step
your swivel is my "little kick"—
something learned not through thoughtful practice
but mindless loyalty
to the *congas y timbales.*
Cuban style, you say, is to rely on your hips
to push with the curve of a lateral *tilde.*
We become equivalence.

Later, *los calles de La Habana* lead me through hisses
and the distinct smell of 1952 carnival-blue Chevrolet jams
or along the Malecón
where a stranger would call to me:
¿Brasileña?
¿Italiana?
¡Ven acá!
I could simply respond with a silent ignorance of an outsider
or say *no, una mestiza, una indigena*
and slowly pronounce *A-ni-shi-na-be*
en el norte de los Estados Unidos.
And it is here, as the waves power toward us from African winds
where slave ships once carved new crowns for Spain,
here, where I see pairs of dancers
swirling the most beautiful bronze into the night
the spray misting us
bringing in centuries of sugarcane money and the business of *ron,*
here, in this moment, he finally says, oh, indian
as he extends his finger on top of his head

an indication of a feather
and I
only nod my head
in recognition
of its ubiquity.

10 Little Indians

An "updated" version of Septimus Winner's 1868 lyrics of Ten Little Injuns
Comic Song and Chorus.

1 traces bloodlines to Anishinaabe grandmothers
      with her right hand,
      French grandfathers with her left.

2 never knows what box to check, used to go mass
      every Sunday in bluejeans and a t-shirt.

3 has blue eyes and an Irish name, wrote her first poem
      in the eighth grade and got a C.

4 occupies two homes, one where she sleeps at night
      and one as memorized landscape, arrowheads
      she found around the bluffs.

5 swims the lakes of her childhood, water she knows by heart,
      has never told the secret of her hands, their sculling.

6 shoots baskets with her brother in the alley
      until the crickets come out.

7 dances salsa and tries to speak Spanish, legs like her
      aunts and grandma;
      she saves the holy cards they send her.

8 helps her mother cook wild rice, her hair pulled into a ponytail,
      has known the recipe, never spoken, since she was small.

9 resists explaining every time someone asks her,
      so, what are you anyway?

10 takes her time, speaks slowly, is careful
      not to be misunderstood.

Dementia

No words now
to lend to a granddaughter
who's relied on them
all her life.

No stories now because
they're boxed up,
trapped
in an urban nursing home.

Stowed for better days
beyond that river dividing
this city and that one.

You carry your same broad
shoulders down halls
unknown to you, navigate

around strangers
in a body that's held
a family through two sons
dying too soon, two others
dying slowly in chemical fogs.

Drifting now, you wade further out
from the shoreline,
holding fast to a horizon
beyond *Misi-ziibi*.

Epilogue

"In order to live we have to make our own mirrors."

— Ojibwe poet Marcie Rendon
from her introduction to the collection of poetry
by four Anishinaabe writers entitled *Nitaawichige*.

If fish tell you something,
listen.
It's not often
water speaks;
rarely do we practice lowering
an ear,
catch the business of swimming.
Here, we are
the charging and refraction;
light stabbing deeper
as you slice with thumb
and index,
body aligned to the nests of Northerns
where anything could happen in these lives.
But it's easier to stand shoreline
throwing ropes out to the drowning
bold, cord-words
absent of song and wild talk.
Instead, tread until your lungs
burn,
you cough and spit water;
scull your hands with the vigor of a river
and never tell anything
but a really good story.

Printed in the USA
CPSIA information can be obtained
at www.ICGtesting.com
LVHW040819250424
778196LV00005B/254